100+ Super Tasty Diet Recipes – 2 Books in 1

Discover the Recipes to Lose Weight while Eating Amazing Dishes

By

Lara Middleton

Sirt Diet Recipes for Dinner

by

Lara Middleton

Additionally, the information in the following pages is intended only for informational purposes and should thus be thought of as universal. As befitting its nature, it is presented without assurance regarding its prolonged validity or interim quality. Trademarks that are mentioned are done without written consent and can in no way be considered an endorsement from the trademark holder.

Table of Contents

Bang-Bang Chicken Noodle Stir-fry

Preparation time: 20 minutes

Cooking time: 1 hour and 10 minutes

Servings: 4

Ingredients:

- 1 tablespoon sunflower oil

- 750g package chicken thighs, boned, any surplus skin trimmed

- 250g frozen chopped mixed peppers

- Inch courgette, peeled into ribbons, seeded center chopped

- 1 chicken stock cube

- 250g pack moderate egg yolks

- 4 garlic cloves, finely chopped
- 1/2 tsp. crushed chilies, and additional to serve (optional)
- 4 tablespoons reduced-salt soy sauce
- 2 tsp. caster sugar
- 1 lime, zested, 1/2 juiced, 1/2 slice into wedges to function

Directions:

- Heat the oil in a skillet on medium-low warmth. Fry the chicken skin-side down to 10 minutes or until your skin is emptied.
- Flip and simmer for 10 minutes, or until cooked. Transfer to a plate cover loosely with foil.
- Reheat the wok over a high temperature, add the peppers and sliced courgette; simmer for 5 minutes.
- Meanwhile, bring a bowl of water to the boil, and then crumble in the stock block, adding the noodles. Simmer for 45 minutes until cooked, and then drain well.
- Insert the garlic and crushed chilies into the wok; simmer for 2 minutes. In a bowl, mix the soy sugar and the lime juice and zest.
- Enhance the wok, bubble 2 minutes; you can add the courgette noodles and ribbons. Toss with tongs to coat in the sauce.

- Cut the chicken into pieces. Divide the noodles between 4 bowls and top with the chicken. Serve with the lime wedges along with extra crushed chilies, in case you prefer.

Nutrition:

- Calories: 710
- Total Fat: 30 g
- Total Carbohydrates: 7 g
- Protein: 40 g

Pesto Salmon Pasta Noodles

Preparation time: 15 minutes

Cooking time: 30 minutes

Servings: 1

Ingredients:

- 350g penne
- 2 x 212g tins cherry salmon, drained
- 1 lemon, zested and juiced
- 190g jar green pesto
- 250g package cherry tomatoes halved
- 100g bunch spring onions, finely chopped
- 125g package reduced-fat mozzarella

Directions:

- Pre heat the oven to 220°C, buff 200°C. Boil the pasta for 5 minutes.

- Drain reserving 100 ml drinking water.

- Mix the salmon, lemon zest, and juice, then pesto, berries and half of the spring onions; season.

- Mix the pasta and reserved cooking water to the dish. Mix the allowed pesto using 1 tablespoon water and then drizzle on the pasta.

- Gently with mozzarella, top it with the rest of the spring onions and bake for 25 minutes until golden.

Nutrition:

- Calories: 281
- Total Fat: 25 g
- Total Carbohydrates: 72 g
- Protein: 43 g

-

Sri Lankan-Style Sweet Potato Curry

Preparation time: 25 minutes

Cooking time: 40 minutes

Servings: 1

Ingredients:

- 1/2 onion, roughly sliced
- 3 garlic cloves, roughly sliced
- 25g sliced ginger, chopped and peeled
- 15g fresh coriander stalks and leaves split leaves sliced
- 2 1/2 tablespoon moderate tikka curry powder
- 60g package cashew nuts
- 1 tablespoon olive oil

- 500g Red mere Farms sweet potatoes, peeled and cut into 3cm balls
- 400ml tin Isle Sun Coconut-milk
- 1/2 vegetable stock block, created as much as 300ml
- 200g Grower's Harvest long-grain rice
- 300g frozen green beans
- 150g Red mere Farms lettuce
- 1 Sun trail Farms lemon, 1/2 juiced, 1/2 cut into wedges to function

Directions:

- Set the onion, ginger, garlic, coriander stalks tikka powder along with half of the cashew nuts in a food processor. Insert 2 tablespoons water and blitz to a chunky paste.
- At a large skillet, warm the oil over moderate heat. Insert the paste and cook, stirring for 5 minutes. Bring the sweet potatoes, stir, and then pour into the coconut milk and stock. Bring to the simmer and boil for 25-35 minutes before the sweet potatoes are tender.
- Meanwhile, cook the rice pack directions. Toast the rest of the cashews at a dry skillet.

- Stir the beans into the curry and then simmer for 2 minutes. Insert the lettuce in handfuls, allowing each to simmer before adding the following; simmer for 1 minute.
- Bring the lemon juice, to taste, & the majority of the coriander leaves. Scatter on the remaining coriander and cashews, then use the rice and lemon wedges.

Nutrition:

- Calories: 747
- Total Fat: 37 g
- Total Carbohydrates: 90 g
- Protein: 14 g

-

Chicken Liver with Tomato Ragu

Preparation time: 15 minutes

Cooking time: 40 minutes

Servings: 4

Ingredients:

- 2 tablespoon olive oil

- 1 onion, finely chopped

- 2 carrots scrubbed and simmer

- 4 garlic cloves, finely chopped

- 1/4 x 30g pack fresh ginger, stalks finely chopped, leaves ripped
- 380g package poultry livers, finely chopped, and almost any sinew removed and lost
- 400g tin Grower's Harvest chopped berries
- 1 chicken stock cube, created around 300ml
- 1/2 tsp. caster sugar
- 300g penne
- 1/4 Sun trail Farms lemon, juiced

Directions:

- On low-medium heat, put 1 tbsp. oil in a large skillet. Fry the onion and carrots to 10 minutes, stirring periodically.
- Stir in the ginger and garlic pops and cook 2 minutes more. Transfer into a bowl set aside.
- Twist the pan into high heat and then add the oil. Bring the chicken livers and simmer for 5 minutes until browned. Pour the onion mix to the pan and then stir in the tomatoes, sugar, and stock.
- Season, bring to the boil, and then simmer for 20 minutes until reduced and thickened and also the liver is cooked through. Meanwhile, cook pasta.

19

- Taste the ragu and put in a second pinch of sugar more seasoning, if needed. Put in a squeeze of lemon juice to taste and stir in two of the ripped basil leaves.
- Divide the pasta between four bowls, then spoon across the ragu and top with the rest of the basil.

Nutrition:

- Calories: 165
- Total Fat: 5 g
- Total Carbohydrates: 1 g
- Protein: 25 g

Minted Lamb with a Couscous Salad

Preparation time: 15 minutes

Cooking time: 15 minutes

Servings: 1

Ingredients:

- 75g Couscous
- 1/2 chicken stock block, composed to 125ml
- 30g pack refreshing flat-leaf parsley, sliced
- 3 mint sprigs, leaves picked and sliced
- 1 tablespoon olive oil
- 200g pack suspended BBQ minted lamb leg beans, De-frosted
- 200g lettuce berries, sliced

- 1/4 tsp., sliced

- 1 spring onion, sliced

- Pinch of ground cumin

- 1/2 lemon, zested and juiced

- 50g reduced-fat salad cheese

Directions:

- Place the couscous into a heatproof bowl and then pour on the inventory. Cover and set aside for 10 minutes, then fluff with a fork and stir in the herbs.

- Meanwhile, rub a little oil within the lamb steaks and season.

- Mix the tomatoes, cucumber and spring onion into the couscous with the oil, the cumin, and lemon juice and zest. Crumble on the salad and serve with the bunny.

Nutrition:

- Calories: 260

- Total Fat: 15 g

- Total Carbohydrates: 5 g

- Protein: 25 g

Jackfruit Tortilla Bowl

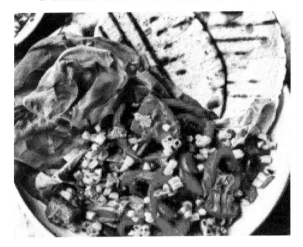

Preparation time: 5 minutes

Cooking time: 15 minutes

Servings: 2

Ingredients:

- 2 Sweet Corn cobettes

- 1 red chili, finely chopped

- 2 teaspoon olive oil

- 1 lime, juiced

- 15g fresh coriander, chopped, plus extra to garnish

- 150g package stained Jack Fruit in Texmex sauce

- 210g tin kidney beans, drained

- 125g roasted red peppers (in the jar), drained and chopped
- 2 whitened tortilla packs
- 1/2 round lettuce, ripped

Directions:

- Heat a griddle Pan on a high temperature (or light a barbecue). Griddle that the cobettes to get 10 -12 minutes, turning until cooked and charred throughout. Remove from the pan and also stand upright onto a plank.
- Use a sharp knife to carefully reduce the span of this corn, staying near to the heart, to clear away the kernels.
- Mix that the kernels with the eucalyptus oil, half of the carrot juice along with half an hour of the coriander.
- Heating the Jack fruit and sauce in a saucepan with the legumes, peppers, staying lime Coriander and juice on medium-low heating for 3 - 4 minutes until heated.
- Griddle the wraps for 10 - 20 seconds each side to char. Tear into pieces and serve together with all the Jack Fruit lettuce and sweet corn salsa.

Nutrition:

- Calories: 390
- Total Fat: 8 g
- Total Carbohydrates: 70 g
- Protein: 13 g

Super-Speedy Prawn Risotto

Preparation time: 10 minutes

Cooking time: 20 minutes

Servings: 4

Ingredients:

- 100g Diced Onion
- 2 X 250g packs whole-grain Rice & Quinoa

- 200g Frozen Garden Peas
- 2 x 150g packs Cooked and Peeled King Prawns
- 1/285g Tote water-cress

Directions:

- Heating 1 tablespoon coconut oil in a skillet on medium-high heat and then put in 100g diced onion; cook for 5 minutes.
- Insert 2 x 250g packs whole-grain Rice & Quinoa along with 175ml hot vegetable stock (or plain water); together side 200g suspended Garden Peas.
- Gently split using rice using a wooden spoon. Cover and cook for 3 minutes, stirring occasionally, you can add two x 150g packs Cooked and Peeled King Prawns.
- Cook for 12 minutes before prawns, peas, and rice have been piping hot, and the majority of the liquid was consumed.
- Remove from heat. Chop 1/2 x 85g tote water-cress and stir throughout; up to taste. Top with watercress leaves and pepper to function.

Nutrition:

- Calories: 347
- Total Fat: 1.4 g
- Cholesterol: 83 g
- Sodium: 398 mg
- Potassium: 322 mg
- Total Carbohydrates: 63 g
- Protein: 18 g

Salmon Burgers

Preparation time: 20 minutes

Cooking time: 15 minutes

Servings: 5

Ingredients:

For Burgers:

- 1 teaspoon olive oil
- 1 cup fresh kale, tough ribs removed and chopped
- 1/3 cup shallots, chopped finely
- Salt and ground black pepper, as required
- 16 ounces skinless salmon fillets
- ¾ cup cooked quinoa
- 2 tablespoons Dijon mustard

- 1 large egg, beaten
- **For Salad:**
- 2½ tablespoons olive oil
- 2½ tablespoons red wine vinegar
- Salt and ground black pepper, as required
- 8 cups fresh baby arugula
- 2 cups cherry tomatoes, halved

Directions:

- For burgers:
- In a large non-stick wok, heat the oil over medium heat and sauté the kale, shallot and kale, salt and black pepper for about 4-5 minutes.
- Remove from heat and transfer the kale mixture into a large bowl. Set aside to cool slightly.
- With a knife, chop 4 ounces of salmon and transfer into the bowl of kale mixture.
- In a food processor, add the remaining salmon and pulse until finely chopped.
- Transfer the finely chopped salmon into the bowl of kale mixture.
- Then, add remaining ingredients and stir until fully combined.

- Make 5 equal-sized patties from the mixture.

- Heat a lightly greased large non-stick wok over medium heat and cook the patties for about 4-5 minutes per side.

- For dressing:

- In a glass bowl, add the oil, vinegar, shallots, salt and black pepper and beat until well combined.

- Add arugula and tomatoes and toss to coat well.

- Divide the salad onto on serving plates and top each with 1 patty.

- Serve immediately.

Nutrition:

- Calories: 329
- Total Fat: 15.8 g
- Saturated Fat: 2.4 g
- Cholesterol: 77 mg
- Sodium: 177 mg
- Total Carbohydrates: 24 g
- Fiber: 3.6 g
- Sugar: 2.7 g
- Protein: 24.9 g

Tofu and Veggies Curry

Preparation time: 20 minutes

Cooking time: 30 minutes

Servings: 1

Ingredients:

- 1 (16-ounce) block firm tofu, drained, pressed and cut into ½-inch cubes
- 2 tablespoons coconut oil
- 1 medium yellow onion, chopped
- 1½ tablespoons fresh ginger, minced
- 2 garlic cloves, minced
- 1 tablespoon curry powder
- Salt and ground black pepper, as required

- 1 cup fresh mushrooms, sliced
- 1 cup carrots, peeled and sliced
- 1 (14-ounce) can unsweetened coconut milk
- ½ cup vegetable broth
- 2 teaspoons light brown sugar
- 10 ounces broccoli florets
- 1 tablespoon fresh lime juice
- ¼ cup fresh basil leaves, sliced thinly

Directions:
- In a Dutch oven, heat the oil over medium heat and sauté the onion, ginger and garlic for about 5 minutes.
- Stir in the curry powder, salt and black pepper and cook for about 2 minutes, stirring occasionally.
- Add the mushrooms and carrot and cook for about 4-5 minutes.
- Stir in the coconut milk, broth and brown sugar and bring to a boil.
- Add the tofu and broccoli and simmer for about 12-15 minutes, stirring occasionally.
- Stir in the lime juice and remove from the heat.
- Serve hot.

Nutrition:

- Calories: 184
- Total Fat: 11.1 g
- Saturated Fat: 6.9 g
- Sodium: 55 mg
- Total Carbohydrates: 14.3 g
- Fiber: 4.5 g
- Sugar: 5 g
- Protein: 10.5 g

Chicken with Veggies

Preparation time: 15 minutes

Cooking time: 25 minutes

Servings: 1

Ingredients:

- 3 tablespoons olive oil

- 1 pound skinless, boneless chicken breast, cubed

- 1 medium onion, chopped

- 6 garlic cloves, minced

- 2 cups fresh mushrooms, sliced

- 16 ounces small broccoli florets

- ¼ cup water
- Salt and ground black pepper, as required

Directions:

- Heat the oil in a large wok over medium heat and cook the chicken cubes for about 4-5 minutes.
- With a slotted spoon, transfer the chicken cubes onto a plate.
- In the same wok, add the onion and sauté for about 4-5 minutes.
- Add the mushrooms and cook for about 4-5 minutes.
- Stir in the cooked chicken, broccoli and water, covered for about 8-10 minutes, stirring occasionally.
- Stir in salt and black pepper and remove from heat.
- Serve hot.

Nutrition:

- Calories: 197
- Total Fat: 10.1 g
- Saturated Fat: 2 g
- Cholesterol: 44 mg
- Sodium: 82 mg
- Total Carbohydrates: 8.5 g
- Fiber: 2.7 g

- Sugar: 2.5 g
- Protein: 20.1 g

Steak with Veggies

Preparation time: 15 minutes

Cooking time: 12 minutes

Servings: 4

Ingredients:

- 2 tablespoons coconut oil
- 4 garlic cloves, minced
- 1 pound beef sirloin steak, cut into bite-sized pieces
- Ground black pepper, as required

- 1½ cups carrots, peeled and cut into matchsticks
- 1½ cups fresh kale, tough ribs removed and chopped
- 3 tablespoons tamari

Directions:

- Melt the coconut oil in a wok over medium heat and sauté the garlic for about 1 minute.
- Add the beef and black pepper and stir to combine.
- Increase the heat to medium-high and cook for about 3-4 minutes or until browned from all sides.
- Add the carrot, kale and tamari and cook for about 4-5 minutes.
- Remove from the heat and serve hot.

Nutrition:

- Calories: 311
- Total Fat: 13.8 g
- Saturated Fat: 8.6 g
- Cholesterol: 101 mg
- Sodium: 700 mg
- Total Carbohydrates: 8.4 g
- Fiber: 1.6 g
- Sugar: 2.3 g

- Protein: 37.1 g

Parsley Lamb Chops with Kale

Preparation time: 25 minutes

Cooking time: 11 minutes

Servings: 4

Ingredients:

- 1 garlic clove, minced
- 1 tablespoon fresh parsley leaves, minced
- Salt and ground black pepper, as required
- 4 lamb loin chops
- 4 cups fresh baby kale

- **Directions:**
- Pre heat the grill to high heat. Grease the grill grate.
- In a bowl, add garlic, rosemary, salt and black pepper and mix well.
- Coat the lamb chops with the herb mixture generously.
- Place the chops onto the hot side of grill and cook for about 2 minutes per side.
- Now, move the chops onto the cooler side of the grill and cook for about 6-7 minutes.
- Divide the kale onto serving plates and top each with 1 chop and serve.

Nutrition:
- Calories: 301
- Total Fat: 10.5 g
- Saturated Fat: 3.8 g
- Cholesterol: 128 mg
- Sodium: 176 mg
- Total Carbohydrates: 7.8 g
- Fiber: 1.4 g
- Protein: 41.9 g

Shrimp with Veggies

Preparation time: 15 minutes

Cooking time: 8 minutes

Servings: 5

Ingredients:

For Sauce

- 1 tablespoon fresh ginger, grated
- 2 garlic cloves, minced
- 3 tablespoons low-sodium soy sauce
- 1 tablespoon red wine vinegar
- 1 teaspoon brown sugar
- ¼ teaspoon red pepper flakes, crushed

41

For Shrimp Mixture

- 3 tablespoons olive oil
- 1½ pounds medium shrimp, peeled and deveined
- 12 ounces broccoli florets
- 8 ounces, carrot, peeled and sliced

Directions:

- For sauce:
- In a bow, place all the ingredients and beat until well combined. Set aside.
- In a large wok, heat oil over medium-high heat and cook the shrimp for about 2 minutes, stirring occasionally.
- Add the broccoli and carrot and cook about 3-4 minutes, stirring frequently.
- Stir in the sauce mixture and cook for about 1-2 minutes.
- Serve immediately.

Nutrition:

- Calories: 298
- Total Fat: 10.7 g
- Saturated Fat: 1.3 g
- Cholesterol: 305 mg

- Sodium: 882 mg

- Total Carbohydrates: 7 g

- Fiber: 2g

- Sugar: 2.4 g

- Protein: 45.5 g

Chickpeas with Swiss chard

Preparation time: 15 minutes

Cooking time: 12 minutes

Servings: 4

Ingredients:

- 2 tablespoon olive oil
- 2 garlic cloves, sliced thinly
- 1 large tomato, chopped finely
- 2 bunches fresh Swiss chard, trimmed
- 1 (18-ounce) can chickpeas, drained and rinsed
- Salt and ground black pepper, as required

- ¼ cup water
- 1 tablespoon fresh lemon juice
- 2 tablespoons fresh parsley, chopped

Directions:

- Heat the oil in a large nonstick wok over medium heat and sauté the garlic for about 1 minute.
- Add the tomato and cook for about 2-3 minutes, crushing with the back f spoon.
- Stir in remaining ingredients except lemon juice and parsley and cook for about 5-7 minutes.
- Drizzle with the lemon juice and remove from the heat.
- Serve hot with the garnishing of parsley.

Nutrition:

- Calories: 217

- Total Fat: 8.3 g

- Sodium: 171 mg

- Total Carbohydrates: 26.2 g

- Fiber: 6.6 g

- Sugar: 1.8 g

- Protein: 8.8 g

Chicken & Berries Salad

Preparation time: 20 minutes

Cooking time: 16 minutes

Servings: 8

Ingredients:

- 2 pounds boneless, skinless chicken breasts
- ½ cup olive oil
- ¼ cup fresh lemon juice
- 2 tablespoons maple syrup
- 1 garlic clove, minced
- Salt and ground black pepper, as required
- 2 cups fresh strawberries, hulled and sliced

- 2 cups fresh blueberries
- 10 cups fresh baby arugula

Directions:

- For marinade: in a large bowl, add oil, lemon juice, Erythritol, garlic, salt and black pepper and beat until well combined.
- In a large re-sealable plastic bag, place the chicken and ¾ cup of marinade.
- Seal bag and shake to coat well.
- Refrigerate overnight.
- Cover the bowl of remaining marinade and refrigerate before serving.
- Preheat the grill to medium heat. Grease the grill grate.
- Remove the chicken from bag and discard the marinade.
- Place the chicken onto grill grate and grill, covered for about 5-8 minutes per side.
- Remove chicken from grill and cut into bite sized pieces.
- In a large bowl, add the chicken pieces, strawberries and spinach and mix.
- Place the reserved marinade and toss to coat.
- Serve immediately.

Nutrition:

- Calories: 377
- Total Fat: 21.5 g
- Cholesterol: 101 mg
- Sodium: 126 mg
- Total Carbohydrates: 12.6 g
- Fiber: 2 g
- Sugar: 9 g
- Protein: 34.1 g

Beef & Kale Salad

Preparation time: 15 minutes

Cooking time: 8 minutes

Servings: 2

Ingredients:

For Steak:

- 2 teaspoons olive oil
- 2 (4-ounce) strip steaks
- Salt and ground black pepper, as required

For Salad:

- ¼ cup carrot, peeled and shredded
- ¼ cup cucumber, peeled, seeded and sliced

- ¼ cup radish, sliced
- ¼ cup cherry tomatoes, halved
- 3 cups fresh kale, tough ribs removed and chopped

For Dressing:
- 1 tablespoon extra-virgin olive oil
- 1 tablespoon fresh lemon juice
- Salt and ground black pepper, as required

Directions:
- For steak:
- In a large heavy-bottomed wok, heat the oil over high heat and cook the steaks with salt and black pepper for about 3-4 minutes per side.
- Transfer the steaks onto a cutting board for about 5 minutes before slicing.
- For salad:
- Place all ingredients in a salad bowl and mix.
- For dressing:
- Place all ingredients in another bowl and beat until well combined.
- Cut the steaks into desired sized slices against the grain.
- Place the salad onto each serving plate.

- Top each plate with steak slices.

- Drizzle with dressing and serve.

Nutrition:

- Calories" 262

- Total Fat: 12 g

- Cholesterol: 63 mg

- Sodium: 506 mg

- Total Carbohydrates: 15.2 g

- Fiber: 2.5g

- Sugar: 3.3 g

- Protein: 25.2 g

Grilled Salmon Fillet with Chilies and Avocado Puree

Preparation time: 10 minutes

Cooking time: 40 minutes

Servings: 3

Ingredients:

2 ripe avocados

- 2 tablespoons of lime juice

- Salt

- Pepper

- 4 fresh salmon fillets of 200 g each

- For the chili sauce:

- 2 chilies
- 4 teaspoons of lime juice
- 4 teaspoons of honey
- 4 spoons of extra virgin olive oil
- 1 large shallot

Directions:

- Cut the two avocados in half and remove the pulp with a teaspoon. Transfer it to the mixer with the lime juice and reduce everything in a silky and homogeneous cream. Salt rule and fresh reel pepper.
- Prepare the sauce by cutting the peppers into rounds, removing the seeds. In a small bowl mix them with the sliced shallot, lime juice, honey and oil. Season with salt and mix well.
- Cook the salmon fillets on a hot cast iron plate for about 4 minutes on the skin side. Turn them over, add a drizzle of oil and complete the cooking according to the thickness.
- Season with salt and pepper, tassel the fillets with the chili sauce and serve immediately with the avocado puree.

Nutrition:

- Calories: 170
- Total Fat: 5 g
- Cholesterol: 70 mg
- Calcium: 20 mg
- Protein: 25 g

Salmon and Capers

Preparation time: 5 minutes

Cooking time: 25 minutes

Servings: 2

Ingredients:

- 75g (3oz) Greek yogurt
- 4 salmon fillets, skin removed
- 4 teaspoons Dijon Mustard
- 1 tablespoon capers, chopped
- 2 teaspoons fresh parsley
- Zest of 1 lemon

Directions:

- In a bowl, mix together the yogurt, mustard, lemon zest, parsley and capers. Thoroughly coat the salmon in the mixture.
- Place the salmon under a hot grill (broiler) and cook for 3-4 minutes on each side, or until the fish is cooked.
- Serve with mashed potatoes and vegetables or a large green leafy salad.

Nutrition:

- Calories: 400
- Total Fat: 23 g
- Cholesterol: 130 mg
- Total Carbohydrates: 3 g
- Protein: 40 g

Asian Slaw

Preparation time: 5 minutes

Cooking time: 25 minutes

Servings: 2

Ingredients:

- 2 cups Red cabbage, shredded
- 2 cups Broccoli florets, chopped
- 1 cup Carrots, shredded
- 1 Red onion, finely sliced
- 1/2 Red bell pepper, finely sliced
- 1/2 Cilantro, chopped
- 1 tbsp. Sesame seeds

- 1/2 Peanuts, chopped
- 2 tsp. Sriracha
- 1/4 Rice wine vinegar
- 1/2 Sesame seed oil
- 1 tsp. Sea salt
- 1 clove Garlic, minced
- 2 tbsp. Peanut butter, natural
- 2 tbsp. extra virgin olive oil
- 2 tbsp. Tamari sauce
- 2 tsp. Ginger, peeled and grated
- 2 tsp. Honey
- 1/4 Black pepper, ground

Directions:
- In a large salad bowl toss the vegetables, cilantro, and peanuts.
- In a smaller bowl, whisk together the remaining ingredients until emulsified. Pour this dressing over the vegetables and toss together until fully coated.
- Chill the slaw for at least ten minutes, so that the flavors meld. Refrigerate the Asian slaw for up to a day in advance for deeper flavors.

Nutrition:

- Calories: 150
- Total Fat: 5 g
- Total Carbohydrates: 10 g
- Protein: 2 g

Egg Fried Buckwheat

Preparation time: 5 minutes

Cooking time: 45 minutes

Servings: 2

Ingredients:

- 2 Eggs, beaten
- 2 tbsp. extra virgin olive oil
- 1 Onion, diced
- 1/2 Peas, frozen
- 2 Carrots, finely diced
- 2 cloves Garlic, minced

- 1 tsp. Ginger, grated

- 2 Green onions, thinly sliced

- 2 tbsp. Tamari sauce

- 2 tsp. Sriracha sauce

- 3 cups cooked buckwheat groats, cold

Directions:

- Add half of the olive oil to a large skillet or set to medium heat then add the egg, stir constantly until it is fully cooked. Remove the egg and transfer it to another dish.

- Add the remaining olive oil to your wok along with the peas, carrots, and onion. Cook until the carrots and onions are softened, about four minutes.

- Add in the grated ginger and minced garlic, cooking for an additional minute until fragrant.

- Add the sriracha sauce, tamari sauce, and cooked buckwheat groats to the wok. Continue to cook the buckwheat groats and stir the mixture until the buckwheat is warmed all the way through and the flavors have melded, about 2 minutes.

- Add the cooked eggs and green onions to the wok, giving it a good toss to combine and serve warm.

Nutrition:

- Calories: 430
- Total Fat: 20 g
- Total Carbohydrates: 30 g
- Protein: 25 g

Sautéed Red Cabbage

Preparation time: 5 minutes

Cooking time: 45 minutes

Servings: 2

Ingredients:

- 1 head small Red cabbage, thinly sliced
- 2 tablespoons extra virgin olive oil
- 1/2 Black pepper, ground
- 1 tbsp. Thyme, fresh, chopped
- 1/2 Apple cider vinegar
- 1 1/2 Sea salt

Directions:

- When slicing your red cabbage into thin ribbons make sure to remove and discard the core.
- Add the extra virgin olive oil to a large skillet with a heavy bottom over medium-high heat. Once warm, add in the red cabbage, sea salt, and pepper.
- Sauté the cabbage until tender and start to brown, about 10 to 15 minutes. You don't need to constantly stir the cabbage, but give it a good stir once every few minutes. By doing this, you will allow the cabbage to caramelize without sticking.
- Remove the cabbage from the heat and stir in the thyme and apple cider vinegar.
- Taste the dish and adjust the seasonings to taste. You might want to even add an extra splash of apple cider vinegar if you will like a little more pop to the dish.

Nutrition:

- Calories: 110
- Total Fat: 1 g
- Protein: 2 g

Kale and Corn Succotash

Preparation time: 5 minutes

Cooking time: 55 minutes

Servings: 2

Ingredients:

- 2 cups Corn kernels
- 1/2 Black pepper, ground
- 2 cups Kale, chopped
- 1 Red onion, finely diced
- 2 cloves Garlic, minced
- 1 cup Grape tomatoes, sliced in half lengthwise
- 1 teaspoon Sea salt

- 2 tablespoons Parsley, chopped
- 1 tablespoon extra-virgin olive oil

Directions:

- Into a large skillet pour the olive oil, red onion, and the corn kernels, sautéing until hot and tender, about four minutes.
- Add the sea salt, garlic, kale, and black pepper to the skillet, cooking until the kale has wilted, about three to five minutes.
- Remove the large skillet from the stove and toss in the parsley and fresh grape tomatoes. Serve warm.

Nutrition:

- Calories: 220
- Total Fat: 11 g
- Protein: 6 g

Baked Vegetables

Preparation time: 5 minutes

Cooking time: 25 minutes

Servings: 2

Ingredients:

- 3 white onions
- 3 large fleshy tomatoes
- 4 spoons of stale breadcrumbs
- Oregano
- Extra virgin olive oil
- Salt

- 4 large potatoes

Directions:

- Prepare the vegetables in the oven by starting to peel and wash the potatoes.
- Dry them and cut them into slices about one centimeter thick. Peel the onions and cut them into slices of the same thickness. Also wash and slice the tomatoes.
- Brush a round baking pan with oil and arrange the vegetables in concentric circles alternating slices of potatoes, onions and tomatoes.
- Sprinkle with breadcrumbs and oregano, season with a drizzle of oil and salt.
- Bake at 170-180 ° for 30 minutes.
- Withdraw vegetables in the oven, let them settle for about ten minutes and serve immediately on the table.

Nutrition:

- Calories: 160
- Total Fat: 5 g
- Total Carbohydrates: 25 g
- Protein: 3 g

Peanut Broccoli Buckwheat Bowls

Preparation time: 5 minutes

Cooking time: 25 minutes

Servings: 2

Ingredients:

- 1 cup Buckwheat, uncooked

- 1 cup Frozen peas, thawed

- 14 ounces Tofu, extra-firm, pressed to remove excess liquid

- 24 ounces Broccoli florets

- 1 Red onion, diced

- 1/4 cup Parsley, chopped

- 1 1/2 Sea salt

- 2 cloves Garlic, minced

The Sauce:

- 1/4 Tamari sauce

- 1/2 Water

- 1/2 Peanut butter, natural sugar-free

- 3 tablespoons Lime juice

- 1 teaspoon Tahini paste

- 1/2 teaspoon Sriracha paste

- 1-inch nob Ginger root, peeled

- 2 cloves Garlic, minced

- 1/2 teaspoon Maple syrup

Directions:

- Pour the water, tamari sauce, and other ingredients for the sauce into a blender and combine it on high speed until completely smooth.

- Adjust the thickness to your taste, adding more water if desired. Taste and adjust the flavors to your preferences. Place the sauce to the side while you assemble the bowls.

- Once you have drained the excess liquid off of the tofu (this is best done with a tofu press) slice the block in half lengthwise, so that you have two rectangular bricks. Slice both bricks of tofu into bite-sized cubes.

- Set the sliced cubes of tofu on a baking sheet and toss them with half of the sea salt, baking them in an oven preheated to a temperature of Fahrenheit 400 degrees until crispy, about 25-30 minutes. Halfway through the cooking process flip the cubes over so that they crisp evenly.

- Cook the buckwheat. Add the two cups of water into a pan and bring it to a boil before stirring in the remaining sea salt and the buckwheat grains.

- Cover with a lid, reduce the heat to medium-low, and allow it to cook until the water is absorbed, about fifteen minutes.

- While the tofu and buckwheat cooks begin preparing the vegetables. Chop the florets of broccoli into bite-size chunks and then add it into a large bowl along with the red onion and the prepared peanut sauce.

- Toss together until the broccoli and onions is coated in the sauce then transfer the vegetables

- Using a large fork fluff the cooked buckwheat and stir in the minced garlic. Divide the buckwheat between bowls for serving, top with the broccoli mixture, and lastly the tofu cubes. Enjoy while warm.

Nutrition:

- Calories: 130
- Total Fat: 7 g
- Total Carbohydrates: 15 g
- Protein: 2 g

Roast Pork Beer with Onions

Preparation time: 5 minutes

Cooking time: 2 hours and 30 minutes

Servings: 1

Ingredients:

- 2 bay leaves
- 3 sprigs of thyme
- 300 ml of light beer
- Extra virgin olive oil
- 30 g of butter
- Salt

- Black pepper

- 1 kg of loin or pork shoulder

- 800 g of blond onions

Directions:

- To make the beer roast pork with onions, start tying the piece of meat with several turns of kitchen string.

- Massage it with a pinch of salt and ground pepper, then brown it in a saucepan with the butter and 4 tablespoons of oil.

- Turn it well on all sides so that the browning takes place uniformly. Take the roast from the saucepan and keep it warm.

- Add the peeled and finely chopped onions, bay leaves and thyme sprigs to the cooking juices.

- Mix well and let gently stew for 5 minutes. Then transfer the onions to an ovenproof dish, add the meat and drizzle everything with the beer.

- Cover with a lid or aluminum foil and transfer the dish to the oven, preheated to 150 ° for 2 hours and 30 minutes.

- After cooking, remove the aromatic herbs and transfer the pork roast to the beer with onions on a serving plate. Serve it sliced with its cooking sauce.

Nutrition:

- Calories: 305
- Total Fat: 21 g
- Cholesterol: 80 mg
- Sodium: 695 mg
- Potassium: 300 mg
- Total Carbohydrates: 7 g
- Protein: 21 g

Quinoa Nut and Radicchio Meatballs

Preparation time: 10 minutes

Cooking time: 50 minutes

Servings: 8

Ingredients:

- 120 grams of white quinoa
- 2 tufts of late-growing radicchio di Treviso
- 80 grams of walnut kernels
- 2 teaspoons of turmeric
- 1 cup of foil flour
- 2 teaspoons of marjoram
- Extra virgin olive oil

- Salt and pepper to taste

Directions:

- Wash the quinoa and boil it in lightly salted water until the seeds open and are soft.
- When the quinoa is cooked, squeeze it well, then add the turmeric and pepper and keep it aside.
- In a centrifuge add the nuts, salt, pepper and radicchio washed, blanched and dried well, and add a drizzle of oil.
- Blend everything until a cream is obtained. Add the quinoa cream.
- With floured hands, form balls from the dough and roll them into a mix of flour and chives.
- Crush the meatballs at the ends. If the dough is too soft, leave it to rest for half an hour or thicken it with a little flour.
- Place the meatballs on a sheet of baking paper sprinkled and bake at 180° for 20 minutes. Halfway through cooking, turn the meatballs to the other side.
- Take them out of the oven and place them on an absorbent sheet to remove excess oil. Serve them hot.

Nutrition:

- Calories: 240
- Total Fat: 8 g
- Cholesterol: 53 mg

- Total Carbohydrates: 27 g

- Protein: 17 g

Chicken Paprika and Vegetables

Preparation time: 15 minutes

Cooking time: 50 minutes

Servings: 4

Ingredients:

- 60 gr of extra virgin olive oil

- 40 grams of paprika

- 2 orange carrots

- Half celeriac

- 3 turnips
- Chicken wings 300 g
- Vegetable broth 1 liter
- Thyme and rosemary
- Fresh bay 2 leaves
- Pepper and salt to taste
- Lemon
- 1 cup of chopped cabbage

Directions:
- Clean and chop celeriac, turnip and carrot.
- In a large pan, heat a drizzle of oil and add the chicken wings, paprika and chopped vegetables, cook for a few minutes.
- Add salt and pepper, thyme and rosemary on the chicken wings and add a ladle of vegetable stock, cover the pan and let it boil.
- When the broth dries add another ladle, and continue cooking the chicken on a low flame for about 40 minutes.
- In the meantime, remove the outer leaves of the cabbage, wash it and chop it up, put it in the pan with the paprika chicken and continue to cook with the help of the stock until the cabbage is cooked.

- Put out the fire, cover and let it rest for a few minutes before serving.

Nutrition:
- Calories: 150
- Total Fat: 2 g
- Cholesterol: 68 mg
- Total Carbohydrates: 4 g
- Protein: 28 g

Buckwheat Burger

Preparation time: 15 minutes

Cooking time: 40 minutes

Servings: 3

Ingredients:

- 200 g Buckwheat without peel

- Pound of red lentils

- 35 g Pumpkin seeds

- 4 tablespoons Baking powder

- 1/2 red onion, Tropia variety

- 1 slice Garlic

- Oregano, thyme or other spices to taste

- Rosemary

- Soy sauce

- Pepper

- Yellow polenta flour

- **Directions:**

- Pour about 600 ml of water into a large pot.

- Clean the onion and cut it thin, mince the garlic and wash the lentils. Put all the ingredients, including the spices, in the pot with water and add the buckwheat.

- Light the fire and cook until all the water is absorbed. When cooking, add the rosemary sprig (which you will remove at the end)

- When cooked, pour everything into a fairly large container, complete by combining the chopped pumpkin seeds and yeast, mix well and let everything cool. With your hands a little oiled, take a small amount of the mixture and form the burger. Pass them in the yellow polenta flour.

- As you prepare them, place them on a baking tray, on which you will have placed the greaseproof baking paper, and bake at 180°. It's half cooked, turn them over and let them cook again. The cooking time is about twenty minutes.

- Alternatively, burgers can cook in a pan with a drizzle of oil for fifteen minutes. Serve the burgers with some arugula.

Nutrition:

- Calories: 185

- Total Fat: 10 g

- Total Carbohydrates: 25 g

- Protein: 9 g

Tofu and Buckwheat Salad

Preparation time: 10 minutes

Cooking time: 20 minutes

Servings: 4

Ingredients:

- 300 g Buckwheat
- 400 gr Cherry tomatoes
- 125 g Natural tofu
- 10 leaves of Basil
- 150 g Sunflower seeds
- Extra virgin olive oil and Salt

Directions:

- Prepare a pot almost full of cold water and put it on the stove.

- Wash the buckwheat carefully under running water, pour it into the pot on the stove and let it cook for about 20 minutes.

- In a large container put some basil leaves washed with care and the tomatoes washed and cut into four pieces.

- Once cooked, drain the buckwheat and cool it under running water.

- Cut the tofu into pieces and add it together with the wheat in the container with the tomatoes.

- Add the remaining basil leaves and sunflower seeds, salt and pepper system and finally add a drizzle of oil, mix everything well and let it rest.

- You can have the salad still warm and freshly made or leave it in the fridge and eat it cold.

Nutrition:

- Calories: 400
- Fat: 10 g
- Carbohydrates: 50 g
- Protein: 20 g

Courgette Tortillas

Preparation time: 5 minutes

Cooking time: 20 minutes

Servings: 4

Ingredients:

- 20 g Butter in chunks or alternatively 2 spoons of coconut oil
- 2 green zucchini
- 4 whole eggs
- Pepper and salt to taste
- Parsley or chives

Directions:

- Wash and slice the zucchini.
- In a high pot, melt the butter or heat the oil. When it is ready, pour in the freshly cut zucchini and stir well until they soften.
- In a bowl break the four eggs, beat them adding salt, pepper, parsley or chives. Pour the mixture over the zucchini.
- Cook until the eggs are almost cooked, before finishing put the pot in the oven and turn on the grill to toast the tortillas.

Nutrition:

- Calories: 97
- Fat: 1 g
- Carbohydrates: 20 g

- Protein: 4 g

Sirt Diet Snacks and Desserts

By

Lara Middleton

Additionally, the information in the following pages is intended only for informational purposes and should thus be thought of as universal. As befitting its nature, it is presented without assurance regarding its prolonged validity or interim quality. Trademarks that are mentioned are done without written consent and can in no way be considered an endorsement from the trademark holder.

Table of Contents

Baby Spinach Snack

Preparation time: 10 minutes

Cooking time: 10 minutes

Servings: 1

Ingredients:

2 cups baby spinach, washed

A pinch of black pepper

½ tablespoon olive oil

½ teaspoon garlic powder

Directions:

Spread the baby spinach on a lined baking sheet, add oil, black pepper and garlic powder, toss a bit.

Bake at 350 degrees F for 10 minutes, divide into bowls and serve as a snack.

Enjoy!

Nutrition:

Calories: 125

Fat: 4 g

Fiber: 1 g

Carbohydrates: 4 g

Protein: 2 g

Sesame Dip

Preparation time: 10 minutes

Cooking time: 0 minutes

Servings: 1

Ingredients:

1 cup sesame seed paste, pure

Black pepper to the taste

1 cup veggie stock

½ cup lemon juice

½ teaspoon cumin, ground

3 garlic cloves, chopped

Directions:

In your food processor, mix the sesame paste with black pepper, stock, lemon juice, cumin and garlic.

Pulse very well, divide into bowls and serve as a party dip.

Enjoy!

Nutrition:

Calories: 120

Fat: 12 g

Fiber: 2 g

Carbohydrates: 7 g

Protein: 4 g

Rosemary Squash Dip

Preparation time: 10 minutes

Cooking time: 40 minutes

Servings: 1

Ingredients:

1 cup butternut squash, peeled and cubed

1 tablespoon water

Cooking spray

2 tablespoons coconut milk

2 teaspoons rosemary, dried

Black pepper to the taste

Directions:

Spread squash cubes on a lined baking sheet, spray some cooking oil, introduce in the oven, bake at 365 degrees F for 40 minutes.

Transfer to your blender, add water, milk, rosemary and black pepper, pulse well, divide into small bowls and serve.

Enjoy!

Nutrition:

Calories: 182

Fat: 5 g

Fiber: 7 g

Carbohydrates: 12 g

Protein: 5 g

Bean Spread

Preparation time: 10 minutes

Cooking time: 6 hours

Servings: 1

Ingredients:

1 cup white beans, dried

1 teaspoon apple cider vinegar

1 cup veggie stock

1 tablespoon water

Directions:

In your slow cooker, mix beans with stock, stir, cover, cook on Low for 6 hours.

Drain and transfer to your food processor, add vinegar and water, pulse well, divide into bowls and serve.

Enjoy!

Nutrition:

Calories: 181

Fat: 6 g

Fiber: 5 g

Carbohydrates: 9 g

Protein: 7 g

Corn Spread

Preparation time: 10 minutes

Cooking time: 10 minutes

Servings: 1

Ingredients:

30 ounces canned corn, drained

2 green onions, chopped

½ cup coconut cream

1 jalapeno, chopped

½ teaspoon chili powder

Directions:

In a small pan, combine the corn with green onions, jalapeno and chili powder, stir, and bring to a simmer.

Cook over medium heat for 10 minutes, leave aside to cool down, add coconut cream, stir well, divide into small bowls and serve as a spread.

Enjoy!

Nutrition:

Calories: 192

Fat: 5

Fiber 10

Carbohydrates: 11 g

Protein: 8 g

Mushroom Dip

Preparation time: 10 minutes

Cooking time: 20 minutes

Servings: 1

Ingredients:

1 cup yellow onion, chopped

3 garlic cloves, minced

1 pound mushrooms, chopped

28 ounces tomato sauce, no-salt-added

Black pepper to the taste

Directions:

Put the onion in a pot, add garlic, mushrooms, black pepper and tomato sauce, and stir.

Cook over medium heat for 20 minutes, leave aside to cool down, divide into small bowls and serve.

Enjoy!

Nutrition:

Calories 215

Fat: 4 g

Fiber: 7 g

Carbohydrates: 3 g

Protein: 7 g

Salsa Bean Dip

Preparation time: 10 minutes

Cooking time: 20 minutes

Servings: 1

Ingredients:

½ cup salsa

2 cups canned white beans, no-salt-added, drained and rinsed

1 cup low-fat cheddar, shredded

2 tablespoons green onions, chopped

Directions:

In a small pot, combine the beans with the green onions and salsa, stir, bring to a simmer over medium heat, and cook for 20 minutes Add cheese, stir until it melts, and take off heat, leave aside to cool down, divide into bowls and serve.

Enjoy!

Nutrition:

Calories: 212

Fat: 5 g

Fiber: 6 g

Carbohydrates: 10 g

Protein: 8 g

Mung Beans Snack Salad

Preparation time: 10 minutes

Cooking time: 0 minutes

Servings: 1

Ingredients:

2 cups tomatoes, chopped

2 cups cucumber, chopped

3 cups mixed greens

2 cups mung beans, sprouted

2 cups clover sprouts

For the salad dressing:

1 tablespoon cumin, ground

1 cup dill, chopped

4 tablespoons lemon juice

1 avocado, pitted, peeled and roughly chopped

1 cucumber, roughly chopped

Directions:

In a salad bowl, mix tomatoes with 2 cups cucumber, greens, clover and mung sprout.

In your blender, mix cumin with dill, lemon juice, 1 cucumber and avocado, blend really well, add this to your salad, toss well and serve as a snack

Enjoy!

Nutrition:

Calories: 120

Fat: 0 g

Fiber: 2 g

Carbohydrates: 1 g

Protein: 6 g

Greek Party Dip

Preparation time: 10 minutes

Cooking time: 0 minutes

Servings: 1

Ingredients:

½ cup coconut cream

1 cup fat-free Greek yogurt

2 teaspoons dill, dried

2 teaspoons thyme, dried

1 teaspoon sweet paprika

2 teaspoons no-salt-added sun-dried tomatoes, chopped

2 teaspoons parsley, chopped

2 teaspoons chives, chopped

Black pepper to the taste

Directions:

In a bowl, mix cream with yogurt, dill with thyme, paprika, tomatoes, parsley, chives and pepper, stir well.

Divide into smaller bowls and serve as a dip.

Enjoy!

Nutrition:

Calories: 100

Fat: 1 g

Fiber: 4 g

Carbohydrates: 8 g

Protein: 3 g

Zucchini Bowls

Preparation time: 10 minutes

Cooking time: 20 minutes

Servings: 12

Ingredients:

Cooking spray

½ cup dill, chopped

1 egg

½ cup whole wheat flour

Black pepper to the taste

1 yellow onion, chopped

2 garlic cloves, minced

3 zucchinis, grated

Directions:

In a bowl, mix zucchinis with garlic, onion, flour, pepper, egg and dill, stir well, shape small bowls out of this mix.

Arrange them on a lined baking sheet; grease them with some cooking spray.

Bake at 400 degrees F for 20 minutes, flipping them halfway, divide them into bowls and serve as a snack.

Enjoy!

Nutrition:

Calories: 120

Fat: 1 g

Fiber: 4 g

Carbohydrates: 12 g

Protein: 6 g

Baking Powder Biscuits

Preparation time: 10 minutes

Cooking time: 10 minutes

Servings: 1 2

Ingredients:

1 egg white

1 c. white whole-wheat flour

4 tbsp. of Non-hydrogenated vegetable shortening

1 tbsp. sugar

2/3 c. low-fat milk

1 c. unbleached all-purpose flour

4 tsps. Sodium-free baking powder

Directions:

Preheat oven to 450°F. Take out a baking sheet and set aside.

118

Place the flour, sugar, and baking powder into a mixing bowl and whisk well to combine.

Cut the shortening into the mixture using your fingers, and work until it resembles coarse crumbs. Add the egg white and milk and stir to combine.

Turn the dough out onto a lightly floured surface and knead 1 minute. Roll dough to ¾ inch thickness and cut into 12 rounds.

Place rounds on the baking sheet. Place baking sheet on middle rack in oven and bake 10 minutes.

Remove baking sheet and place biscuits on a wire rack to cool.

Nutrition:

Calories: 118

Fat: 4 g

Carbohydrates: 16 g

Protein: 3 g

Sugars: 0.2 g

Sodium: 294 mg

Vegan Rice Pudding

Preparation time: 5 minutes

Cooking time: 20 minutes

Servings: 8

Ingredients:

½ tsp. ground cinnamon

1 c. rinsed basmati

1/8 tsp. ground cardamom

¼ c. sugar

1/8 tsp. pure almond extract

1 quart vanilla nondairy milk

1 tsp. pure vanilla extract

Directions:

Measure all of the ingredients into a saucepan and stir well to combine. Bring to a boil over medium-high heat.

Once boiling, reduce heat to low and simmer, stirring very frequently, about 15–20 minutes.

Remove from heat and cool. Serve sprinkled with additional ground cinnamon if desired.

Nutrition:

Calories: 148

Fat: 2 g

Carbohydrates: 26 g

Protein: 4 g

Sugars: 35 g

Sodium: 150 mg

Orange and Carrots

Preparation time: 5 minutes

Cooking time: 25 minutes

Servings: 1

Ingredients:

1 pound carrots, peeled and roughly sliced

1 yellow onion, chopped

1 tablespoon olive oil

Zest of 1 orange, grated

Juice of 1 orange

1 orange, peeled and cut into segments

1 tablespoon rosemary, chopped

A pinch of salt and black pepper

Directions:

Heat up a pan with the oil over medium-high heat.

Add the onion and sauté for 5 minutes.

Add the carrots, the orange zest and the other ingredients.

Cook over medium heat for 20 minutes more, divide between plates and serve.

Nutrition:

Calories: 140

Fat: 3.9 g

Fiber: 5 g

Carbohydrates: 26.1 g

Protein: 2.1 g

Baked Broccoli and Pine Nuts

Preparation time: 10 minutes

Cooking time: 30 minutes

Servings: 1

Ingredients:

2 tablespoons olive oil

1 pound broccoli florets

1 tablespoon garlic, minced

1 tablespoon pine nuts, toasted

1 tablespoon lemon juice

2 teaspoons mustard

A pinch of salt and black pepper

Directions:

In a roasting pan, combine the broccoli with the oil, the garlic and the other ingredients, toss and bake at 380 degrees F for 30 minutes. Divide everything between plates and serve as snack.

Nutrition:

Calories: 220

Fat: 6 g

Fiber: 2 g

Carbohydrates: 7 g

Protein: 6 g

Turmeric Carrots

Preparation time: 10 minutes

Cooking time: 40 minutes

Servings: 1

Ingredients:

1 pound baby carrots, peeled

1 tablespoon olive oil

2 spring onions, chopped

2 tablespoons balsamic vinegar

2 garlic cloves, minced

1 teaspoon turmeric powder

1 tablespoon chives, chopped

¼ teaspoon cayenne pepper

A pinch of salt and black pepper

Directions:

Spread the carrots on a baking sheet lined with parchment paper, add the oil, the spring onions and the other ingredients, toss and bake at 380 degrees F for 40 minutes.

Divide the carrots between plates and serve.

Nutrition:

Calories: 79

Fat: 3.8 g

Fiber: 3.7 g

Carbohydrates: 10.9 g

Protein: 1 g

Hawaii Salad

Preparation time: 10 minutes

Cooking time: 15 minutes

Servings: 1

Ingredients:

1 hand Arugula

1 / 2 pieces Red onion

1 piece winter carrot

2 pieces Pineapple slices

80 g Diced ham

1 pinch Salt

1 pinch Black pepper

Directions:

Cut the red onion into thin half rings.

Remove the peel and hard core from the pineapple and cut the pulp into thin pieces.

Clean the carrot and use a spiralizer to make strings.

Mix rocket and carrot in a bowl. Spread this over a plate.

Spread the red onion, pineapple and diced ham over the rocket.

Drizzle olive oil and balsamic vinegar on the salad to your taste.

Season it with salt and pepper.

Nutrition:

Calories: 150

Total Fat: 2.8 g

Cholesterol: 2 mg

Sodium: 42 mg

Potassium: 172 mg

Carbohydrates: 23 g

Protein: 2 g

Fresh Salad with Orange Dressing

Preparation time: 10 minutes

Cooking time: 15 minutes

Servings: 1

Ingredients:

1 / 2 fruit Salad

1 piece yellow bell pepper

1 piece Red pepper

100 g Carrot (grated)

1 hand Almonds

Dressing:

4 tablespoon Olive oil

110 ml Orange juice (fresh)

1 tablespoon Apple cider vinegar

Directions:

Clean the peppers and cut them into long thin strips.

Tear off the lettuce leaves and cut them into smaller pieces.

Mix the salad with the peppers and the carrots processed in a bowl.

Roughly chop the almonds and sprinkle over the salad.

Mix all the ingredients for the dressing in a bowl.

Pour the dressing over the salad just before serving.

Nutrition:

Calories: 46.6

Total Fat: 0.1 g

Sodium: 230.8 mg

Potassium: 35.6 mg

Total Carbohydrates: 5.6 g

Protein: 0.7 g

Sweet Potato Hash Brown

Preparation time: 5 minutes

Cooking time: 15 minutes

Servings: 2

Ingredients:

1 pinch Celtic sea salt

1 tablespoon Coconut oil

2 pieces Sweet potato

2 pieces Red onion

2 teaspoons Balsamic vinegar

1 piece Apple

125 g lean bacon strips

Directions:

Clean the red onions and cut them into half rings.

Heat a pan with a little coconut oil over medium heat. Fry the onion until it's almost done.

Add the balsamic vinegar and a pinch of salt and cook until the balsamic vinegar has boiled down. Put aside.

Peel the sweet potatoes and cut them into approx. 1.5 cm cubes.

Heat the coconut oil in a pan and fry the sweet potato cubes for 10 minutes.

Add the bacon strips for the last 2 minutes and fry them until you're done.

Cut the apple into cubes and add to the sweet potato cubes. Let it roast for a few minutes.

Then add the red onion and stir well.

Spread the sweet potato hash browns on 2 plates.

Nutrition:

Calories: 101

Total Fat: 7 g

Sodium: 5 mg

Potassium: 97 mg

Carbohydrates: 9 g

Protein: 0.8 g

Herby French Fries with Herbs and Avocado Dip

Preparation time: 15 minutes

Cooking time: 35 minutes

Servings: 1

Ingredient:

For the Fries:

1 / 2 pieces Celery

150 g Sweet potato

1 teaspoon dried oregano

1 / 2 teaspoon Dried basil

1 / 2 teaspoon Celtic sea salt

1 teaspoon Black pepper

1 1 / 2 tablespoon Coconut oil (melted)

Baking paper sheet

For the avocado dip:

1 piece Avocado

4 tablespoons Olive oil

1 tablespoon Mustard

1 teaspoon Apple cider vinegar

1 tablespoon Honey

2 cloves Garlic (pressed)

1 teaspoon dried oregano

Directions:

Preheat the oven to 205 ° C.

Peel the celery and sweet potatoes.

Cut the celery and sweet potatoes into (thin) French fries.

Place the French fries in a large bowl and mix with the coconut oil and herbs.

Shake the bowl a few times so that the fries are covered with a layer of the oil and herb mixture.

Place the chips in a layer on a baking sheet lined with baking paper or on a grill rack.

Bake for 25-35 minutes (turn over after half the time) until they have a nice golden brown color and are crispy.

For the avocado dip:

Puree all ingredients evenly with a hand blender or blender.

Nutrition:

Calories: 459

Total Fat: 27 g

Total Carbohydrates: 50 g

Protein: 4 g

Spiced Burger

Preparation time: 20 minutes

Cooking time: 30 minutes

Serving: 1

Ingredients:

Ground beef 250 g

1 clove Garlic

1 teaspoon dried oregano

1 teaspoon Paprika powder

1 / 2 tsp. Caraway ground

Ingredients toppings:

4 pieces Mushrooms

1 piece Little Gem

1 / 4 pieces Zucchini

1 / 2 pieces Red onion

1 piece Tomato

Directions:

Squeeze the clove of garlic.

Mix all the ingredients for the burgers in a bowl. Divide the mixture into two halves and crush the halves into hamburgers.

Place the burgers on a plate and put in the fridge for a while.

Cut the zucchini diagonally into 1 cm slices.

Cut the red onion into half rings. Cut the tomato into thin slices and cut the leaves of the Little Gem salad.

Grill the hamburgers on the grill until they're done.

Place the mushrooms next to the burgers and grill on both sides until cooked but firm.

Place the zucchini slices next to it and grill briefly.

Now it's time to build the burger: Place 2 mushrooms on a plate then stack the lettuce, a few slices of zucchini and tomatoes. Then put the burger on top and finally add the red onion.

Nutrition:

Calories: 158

Fat: 8 g

Total Carbohydrates: 17 g

Protein: 3 g

Ganache Squares

Preparation time: 15 minutes

Cooking time: 2 hours and 20 minutes

Servings: 10

Ingredients:

250 ml Coconut milk (can)

1 1/2 tablespoon Coconut oil

100 g Honey

1/2 teaspoon Vanilla extract

350 g pure chocolate (70% cocoa)

1 pinch Salt

2 hands Pecans

Directions:

Place the coconut milk in a saucepan and heat for 5 minutes over medium heat.

Add the vanilla extract, coconut oil and honey and cook for 15 minutes. Add a pinch of salt and stir well.

Break the chocolate into a bowl and pour the hot coconut milk over it. Keep stirring until all of the chocolate has dissolved in the coconut milk.

In the meantime, roughly chop the pecans. Heat a pan without oil and roast the pecans.

Stir the pecans through the ganache.

Let the ganache cool to room temperature. (You may be able to speed this up by placing the bowl in a bowl of cold water.)

Line a baking tin with a sheet of parchment paper. Pour the cooled ganache into it.

Place the ganache in the refrigerator for 2 hours to allow it to harden. When the ganache has hardened, you can take it out of the mold and cut it into the desired shape.

Nutrition:

Calories: 141

Fat: 11 g

Carbohydrates: 9 g

Protein: 1 g

Date Candy

Preparation time: 20 minutes

Cooking time: 3 – 4 hours

Servings: 10

Ingredients:

10 pieces Medjool dates

1 hand Almonds

100 g pure chocolate (70% cocoa)

2 1/2 tablespoon Grated coconut

Directions:

Melt chocolate in a water bath.

Roughly chop the almonds.

In the meantime, cut the dates lengthways and take out the core.

143

Fill the resulting cavity with the roughly chopped almonds and close the dates again.

Place the dates on a sheet of parchment paper and pour the melted chocolate over each date.

Sprinkle the grated coconut over the chocolate dates.

Place the dates in the fridge so the chocolate can harden.

Nutrition:

100% joy!

Paleo Bars with Dates and Nuts

Preparation time: 10 minutes

Cooking time: 15 minutes

Servings: 16

Ingredients:

180 g Dates

60 g Almonds

60 g Walnuts

50 g Grated coconut

1 teaspoon Cinnamon

Directions:

Roughly chop the dates and soak them in warm water for 15 minutes.

In the meantime, roughly chop the almonds and walnuts.

Drain the dates.

Place the dates with the nuts, coconut and cinnamon in the food processor and mix to an even mass. (But not too long, crispy pieces or nuts make it particularly tasty)

Roll out the mass on 2 baking trays to form an approximately 1 cm thick rectangle.

Cut the rectangle into bars and keep each bar in a piece of parchment paper.

Nutrition:

Calories: 227

Total Fat: 19 g

Sodium: 9 mg

Carbohydrates: 12 g

Protein: 5 g

Hazelnut Balls

Preparation time: 20 minutes

Cooking time: 4 – 5 hours

Servings: 10

Ingredients:

130 g Dates

140 g Hazelnuts

2 tablespoon Cocoa powder

1 / 2 teaspoon Vanilla extract

1 teaspoon Honey

Directions:

147

Put the hazelnuts in a food processor and grind them until you get hazelnut flour (you can also use ready-made hazelnut flour).

Put the hazelnut flour in a bowl and set aside.

Put the dates in the food processor and grind them until you get a ball.

Add the hazelnut flour, vanilla extract, cocoa and honey and pulse until you get a nice and even mix.

Remove the mixture from the food processor and turn it into beautiful balls.

Store the balls in the fridge.

Nutrition:

Calories: 73

Total Fat: 5 g

Total Carbohydrates: 5 g

Protein: 1 g

Pine and Sunflower Seed Rolls

Preparation time: 20 minutes

Cooking time: 35 minutes

Servings: 10

Ingredients:

120 g Tapioca flour

1 teaspoon Celtic sea salt

4 tablespoon Coconut flour

120 ml Olive oil

120 ml Water (warm)

1 piece Egg (beaten)

150 g Pine nuts (roasted)

150 g Sunflower seeds (roasted)

Baking paper sheet

Directions:

Preheat the oven to 160 ° C.

Put the pine nuts and sunflower seeds in a small bowl and set aside.

Mix the tapioca with the salt and tablespoons of coconut flour in a large bowl. Pour the olive oil and warm water into the mixture.

Add the egg and mix until you get an even texture. If the dough is too thin, add 1 tablespoon of coconut flour at a time until it has the desired consistency.

Wait a few minutes between each addition of the flour so that it can absorb the moisture. The dough should be soft and sticky.

With a wet tablespoon, take tablespoons of batter to make a roll. Put some tapioca flour on your hands so the dough doesn't stick. Fold the dough with your fingertips instead of rolling it in your palms.

Place the roll in the bowl of pine nuts and sunflower seeds and roll it around until covered.

Line a baking sheet with parchment paper. Place the buns on the baking sheet.

Bake in the preheated oven for 35 minutes and serve warm.

Nutrition:

Calories: 163

Total Fat: 14 g

Fiber: 3 g

Total Carbohydrates: 6.5 g

Protein: 5 g

Banana Dessert

Preparation time: 5 minutes

Cooking time: 4 minutes

Servings: 2

Ingredients:

2 pieces Banana (ripe)

2 tablespoons pure chocolate (70% cocoa)

2 tablespoons Almond leaves

Directions:

152

Chop the chocolate finely, cut the banana lengthwise, but not completely, as the banana must serve as a casing for the chocolate.

Slightly slide on the banana, spread the finely chopped chocolate and almonds over the bananas.

Fold a kind of boat out of the aluminum foil that supports the banana well, with the cut in the banana facing up.

Place the two packets and grill them for about 4 minutes until the skin is dark.

Nutrition:

Calories: 105

Total Fat: 0.4 g

Sodium: 1.2 mg

Total Carbohydrates: 27 g

Protein: 1.3 g

Fiber: 3 g

Strawberry Popsicles with Chocolate Dip

Preparation time: 20 minutes

Cooking time: 5 – 6 hours

Servings: 4

Ingredients:

125 g Strawberries

80 ml Water

100 g pure chocolate (70% cocoa)

Directions:

154

Clean the strawberries and cut them into pieces. Puree the strawberries with the water.

Pour the mixture into the Popsicle mold and put it in a skewer.

Place the molds in the freezer so the popsicles can freeze hard.

Once the popsicles are frozen hard, you can melt the chocolate in a water bath.

Dip the popsicles in the melted chocolate mixture.

Nutrition:

Calories: 60

Fiber: 1 g

Sugars: 14 g

Total Carbohydrates: 15 g

Strawberry and Coconut Ice Cream

Preparation time: 20 minutes

Cooking time: 1 hour

Servings: 1

Ingredients:

400 ml Coconut milk (can)

1 hand Strawberries

1 / 2 pieces Lime

3 tablespoons Honey

Directions:

156

Clean the strawberries and cut them into large pieces.

Grate the lime, 1 teaspoon of lime peel is required. Squeeze the lime.

Put all ingredients in a blender and puree everything evenly.

Pour the mixture into a bowl and put it in the freezer for 1 hour.

Take the mixture out of the freezer and put it in the blender. Mix them well again.

Pour the mixture back into the bowl and freeze it until it is hard.

Before serving; take it out of the freezer about 10 minutes before scooping out the balls.

Nutrition:

Calories: 200

Total Fat: 11 g

Cholesterol: 0 mg

Sodium: 5 mg

Total Carbohydrates: 23 g

Protein: 1 g

Coffee Ice Cream

Preparation time: 15 minutes

Cooking time: 1 hour

Servings: 1

Ingredients:

180 ml Coffee

8 pieces Medjool dates

400 ml Coconut milk (can)

1 teaspoon Vanilla extract

Directions:

Make sure that the coffee has cooled down before using it.

Cut the dates into rough pieces.

Place the dates and coffee in a food processor and mix to an even mass.

Add coconut milk and vanilla and puree evenly.

Pour the mixture into a bowl and put it in the freezer for 1 hour.

Take the mixture out of the freezer and scoop it into the blender.

Pour it back into the bowl and freeze it until it's hard.

When serving; take it out of the freezer a few minutes before scooping ice cream balls with a spoon.

Nutrition:

Calories: 140

Total Fat: 7 g

Cholesterol: 25 mg

Sodium: 35 mg

Carbohydrates: 16 g

Banana Strawberry Milkshake

Preparation time: 10 minutes

Cooking time: 10 minutes

Servings: 1

Ingredients:

2 pieces Banana (frozen)

1 hand Strawberries (frozen)

250 ml Coconut milk (can)

Directions:

Peel the bananas, slice them and place them in a bag or on a tray. Put them in the freezer the night before.

Put all ingredients in the blender and mix to an even milkshake.

Spread on the glasses.

Nutrition:

Calories: 110

Total Fat: 1 g

Cholesterol: 5 mg

Sodium: 40 mg

Carbohydrates: 23 g

Sugar: 16 g

Protein: 4 g

Lime and Ginger Green Smoothie

Preparation time: 5 minutes

Cooking time: 5 minutes

Servings: 1

Ingredients:

½ cup dairy free milk

½ cup water

½ teaspoon fresh ginger

½ cup mango chunks

Juice from 1 lime

1 tablespoon dried shredded coconut

1 tablespoon flaxseeds

1 cup spinach

Directions:

Blend together all the ingredients until smooth.

Serve and enjoy!

Nutrition:

Calories 178

Fat 1g

Carbohydrates 7g

Protein 4g

Turmeric Strawberry Green Smoothie

Preparation time: 5 minutes

Cooking time: 5 minutes

Servings: 1

Ingredients:

1 cup kale, stalks removed

1 teaspoon turmeric

1 cup strawberries

½ cup coconut yogurt

6 walnut halves

1 tablespoon raw cacao powder

1-2 mm slice of bird's eye chili

1 cup unsweetened almond milk

1 pitted Medjool date

Directions:

Blend together all the ingredients and enjoy immediately!

Be careful how much almond milk you add so you can choose your favorite consistency.

Nutrition:

Calories 180

Fat 2.2g

Carbohydrates 12g

Protein 4g

Sirtfood Wonder Smoothie

Preparation time: 5 minutes

Cooking time: 10 minutes

Servings: 1

Ingredients:

1 cup arugula (rocket)

2 cups organic strawberries or blueberries

1 cup kale

½ teaspoon matcha green tea

Juice of ½ lemon or lime

3 sprigs of parsley

½ cup of watercress

¾ cup of water

Directions:

Add all the ingredients except matcha to a blender and whizz up until very smooth.

Add the matcha green tea powder and give it a final blitz until well mixed.

Nutrition:

Calories 145

Fat 2g

Carbohydrates 7g

Protein 3g

Strawberry Spinach Smoothie

Preparation time: 5 minutes

Cooking time: 5 minutes

Servings: 1

Ingredients:

1 cup whole frozen strawberries

3 cups packed spinach

¼ cup frozen pineapple chunks

1 medium ripe banana, cut into chunks and frozen

1 cup unsweetened milk

1 tablespoon chia seeds

Directions:

Place all the ingredients in a high-powered blender.

168

Blend until smooth.

Enjoy!

Nutrition:

Calories 266

Fat 8g

Carbohydrates 48g

Protein 9g

Berry Turmeric Smoothie

Preparation time: 5 minutes

Cooking time: 5 minutes

Servings: 1

Ingredients:

1 ½ cups frozen mixed berries (blueberries, blackberries and raspberries)

½ teaspoon ground turmeric

2 cups baby spinach

¾ cup unsweetened vanilla almond milk, or milk of choice

½ cup non-fat plain Greek yogurt, or yoghurt of choice

¼ teaspoon ground ginger

2-3 teaspoons honey

3 tablespoons old-fashioned rolled oats

Directions:

Place all the ingredients in a high-powered blender.

Blend until smooth.

Taste and adjust sweetness as desired.

Enjoy immediately!

Nutrition:

Calories 151

Fat 2g

Carbohydrates 27g

Protein 8g

Mango Green Smoothie

Preparation time: 3 minutes

Cooking time: 5 minutes

Servings: 1

Ingredients:

1 ½ cups frozen mango pieces

1 cup packed baby spinach leaves

1 ripe banana

¾ cup unsweetened vanilla almond milk

Directions:

Place all the ingredients in a blender.

Blend until smooth.

Enjoy!

Nutrition:

Calories 229

Fat 2g

Carbohydrates 72g

Protein 2g

Apple Avocado Smoothie

Preparation time: 5 minutes

Cooking time: 5 minutes

Servings: 1

Ingredients:

2 cups packed spinach

½ medium avocados

1 medium apple, peeled and quartered

½ medium bananas, cut into chunks and frozen

½ cup unsweetened almond milk

1 teaspoon honey

¼ teaspoon ground ginger

Small handful of ice cubes

Directions:

In the ordered list, add the almond milk, spinach, avocado, banana, apples, honey, ginger, and ice to a high-powered blender.

Blend until smooth.

Taste and adjust sweetness and spices as desired.

Enjoy immediately!

Nutrition:

Calories 206

Fat 11g

Carbohydrates 15g

Protein 5g

Kale Pineapple Smoothie

Preparation time: 5 minutes

Cooking time: 5 minutes

Servings: 1

Ingredients:

2 cups lightly packed chopped kale leaves, stems removed

¼ cup frozen pineapple pieces

1 frozen medium banana, cut into chunks

¼ cup non-fat Greek yogurt

2 teaspoons honey

¾ cup unsweetened vanilla almond milk, or any milk of choice

2 tablespoons peanut butter, creamy or crunchy

Directions:

Place all the ingredients in a blender.

Blend until smooth.

Add more milk as needed to reach desired consistency.

Enjoy immediately!

Nutrition:

Calories 187

Fat 9g

Carbohydrates 27g

Protein 8g

Blueberry Banana Avocado Smoothie

Preparation time: 10 minutes

Cooking time: 10 minutes

Servings: 1

Ingredients:

1 medium ripe banana, peeled

2 cups frozen blueberries

1 cup fresh spinach

1 tablespoon ground flaxseed meal

½ ripe avocados

1 tablespoon almond butter

¼ teaspoon cinnamon

½ cup unsweetened vanilla almond milk

Directions:

Place all the ingredients in your blender in the ordered list: vanilla almond milk, spinach, banana, avocado, blueberries, flaxseed meal, and almond butter.

Blend until smooth.

If you like a thicker smoothie, add a small handful of ice.

Enjoy immediately!

Nutrition:

Calories 298

Fat 14.4g

Carbohydrates 38.1g

Protein 8g

Carrot Smoothie

Preparation time: 10 minutes

Cooking time: 10 minutes

Servings: 1

Ingredients:

1 cup chopped carrots

¼ cup frozen diced pineapple

½ cup frozen sliced banana

¼ teaspoon cinnamon

1 tablespoon flaked coconut

½ cup Greek yogurt

2 tablespoons toasted walnuts

Pinch nutmeg

½ cup unsweetened vanilla almond milk, or milk of choice

For topping:

Shredded carrots, coconut, crushed walnuts

Directions:

Add all the ingredients into a blender.

Blend until smooth.

Enjoy immediately, topped with additional shredded carrots, coconut, and crushed walnuts as desired!

Nutrition:

Calories 279

Fat 6g

Carbohydrates 48g

Protein 7g

Matcha Berry Smoothie

Preparation time: 5 minutes

Cooking time: 5 minutes

Servings: 1

Ingredients:

½ bananas

½-tablespoon matcha powder

1 cup almond milk

1 cup frozen blueberries

¼ teaspoon ground ginger

½ tablespoon chia seeds

¼ teaspoon ground cinnamon

Directions:

In a blender, blend the almond milk, banana, blueberries, matcha powder, chia seeds, cinnamon, and ginger until smooth.

Enjoy immediately!

Nutrition:

Calories 212

Fat 5g

Carbohydrates 34g

Protein 8g

Simple Grape Smoothie

Preparation time: 5 minutes

Cooking time: 5 minutes

Servings: 1

Ingredients:

2 cups red seedless grapes

¼ cup grape juice

½ cup plain yogurt

1 cup ice

Directions:

Add grape juice to the blender. Then add yogurt and grapes. Add the ice last.

Blend until smooth and enjoy!

Nutrition:

Calories 161

Fat 4g

Carbohydrates 39g

Protein 2g

Ginger Plum Smoothie

Preparation time: 5 minutes

Cooking time: 5 minutes

Servings: 1

Ingredients:

1 ripe plum, fresh or frozen, pitted but not peeled

½ cup plain yogurt

½ cup orange juice, or other fruit juice

1 teaspoon grated fresh ginger

Directions:

Put all the ingredients in a blender and blend until smooth.

Serve immediately and enjoy!

Nutrition:

Calories 124

Fat 2g

Carbohydrates 26g

Protein 3g

Kumquat Mango Smoothie

Preparation time: 10 minutes

Cooking time: 5 minutes

Servings: 1

Ingredients:

15 small kumquats

½ mango, peeled and chopped

¾ cup unsweetened almond milk

¼ teaspoon vanilla

½ cup plain yogurt

¼ teaspoon nutmeg

1 tablespoon honey

½ teaspoon ground cinnamon

5 ice cubes

Directions:

Cut the kumquats in half and remove any seeds.

Add all the ingredients to a blender and blend until smooth.

Garnish with another sprinkling of cinnamon, if desired.

Enjoy immediately!

Nutrition:

Calories 116

Fat 2g

Carbohydrates 22g

Protein 5g

Cranberry Smoothie

Preparation time: 5 minutes

Cooking time: 5 minutes

Servings: 1

Ingredients:

½ cup frozen cranberries

½ bananas

¼ cup orange juice

¼ cup frozen blueberries

¼ cup low fat Greek yogurt

Directions:

Add all the ingredients to a blender and blend until smooth.

190

Add a little more orange juice if you prefer it a little thinner. Enjoy immediately!

Nutrition:

Calories 165

Fat 1g

Carbohydrates 31g

Protein 8g

Summer Berry Smoothie

Preparation time: 10 minutes

Cooking time: 10 minutes

Servings: 1

Ingredients:

50g (2oz) blueberries

50g (2oz) strawberries

25g (1oz) blackcurrants

25g (1oz) red grapes

1 carrot, peeled

1 orange, peeled

Juice of 1 lime

Directions:

Place all of the ingredients into a blender and cover them with water.

Blitz until smooth.

You can also add some crushed ice and a mint leaf to garnish.

Nutrition:

Calories: 110

Fat: 1 g

Carbohydrates: 20 g

Protein: 2 g

Mango, Celery and Ginger Smoothie

Preparation time: 10 minutes

Cooking time: 10 minutes

Servings: 1

Ingredients:

1 stalk of celery

50g (2oz) kale

1 apple, cored

50g (2oz) mango, peeled, de-stoned and chopped

2.5cm (1 inch) chunk of fresh ginger root, peeled and chopped

Directions:

194

Put all the ingredients into a blender with some water and blitz until smooth. Add ice to make your smoothie really refreshing.

Nutrition:

Calories: 92

Fat: 3 g

Carbohydrates: 22 g

Protein: 1 g

Orange, Carrot and Kale Smoothie

Preparation time: 5 minutes

Cooking time: 5 minutes

Servings: 1

Ingredients:

1 carrot, peeled

1 orange, peeled

1 stick of celery

1 apple, cored

50g (2oz) kale

½ teaspoon matcha powder

Directions:

Place all of the ingredients into a blender and add in enough water to cover them. Process until smooth, serve and enjoy.

Nutrition:

Calories: 150

Fat: 1 g

Carbohydrates: 36 g

Protein: 4 g

Creamy Strawberry and Cherry Smoothie

Preparation time: 5 minutes

Cooking time: 5 minutes

Servings: 1

Ingredients:

100g (3½ oz) strawberries

75g (3oz) frozen pitted cherries

1 tablespoon plain full-fat yogurt

175mls (6fl oz) unsweetened soya milk

Directions:

Place all of the ingredients into a blender and process until smooth. Serve and enjoy.

Nutrition:

Calories: 135

Fat: 1 g

Carbohydrates: 25 g

Protein: 3 g

Pineapple and Cucumber Smoothie

Preparation time: 5 minutes

Cooking time: 5 minutes

Servings: 1

Ingredients:

50g (2oz) cucumber

1 stalk of celery

2 slices of fresh pineapple

2 sprigs of parsley

½ teaspoon matcha powder

Squeeze of lemon juice

Directions:

Place all of the ingredients into blender with enough water to cover them and blitz until smooth.

Nutrition:

Calories: 125

Fat: 1 g

Carbohydrates: 22 g

Protein: 2 g

Avocado, Celery and Pineapple Smoothie

Preparation time: 5 minutes

Cooking time: 5 minutes

Servings: 1

Ingredients:

50g (2oz) fresh pineapple, peeled and chopped

3 stalks of celery

1 avocado, peeled & de-stoned

1 teaspoon fresh parsley

½ teaspoon matcha powder

Juice of ½ lemons

Directions:

Place all of the ingredients into a blender and add enough water to cover them - process until creamy and smooth.

Nutrition:

Calories: 138

Fat: 2 g

Carbohydrates: 25 g

Protein: 5g

Mango and Rocket (Arugula) Smoothie

Preparation time: 5 minutes

Cooking time: 5 minutes

Servings: 1

Ingredients:

25g (1oz) fresh rocket (arugula)

150g (5oz) fresh mango, peeled, de-stoned and chopped

1 avocado, de-stoned and peeled

½ teaspoon matcha powder

Juice of 1 lime

Directions:

Place all of the ingredients into a blender with enough water to cover them and process until smooth. Add a few ice cubes and enjoy.

Nutrition:

Calories: 145

Fat: 2 g

Carbohydrates: 21 g

Protein: 5 g

Strawberry and Citrus Blend

Preparation time: 5 minutes

Cooking time: 5 minutes

Servings: 1

Ingredients:

75g (3oz) strawberries

1 apple, cored

1 orange, peeled

½ avocado, peeled and de-stoned

½ teaspoon matcha powder

Juice of 1 lime

Directions:

Place all of the ingredients into a blender with enough water to cover them and process until smooth. Add ice to make it really refreshing.

Nutrition:

Calories: 112

Fat: 2 g

Carbohydrates: 23 g

Protein: 1 g

Orange and Celery Crush

Preparation time: 5 minutes

Cooking time: 5 minutes

Servings: 1

Ingredients:

1 carrot, peeled

3 stalks of celery

1 orange, peeled

½ teaspoon matcha powder

Juice of 1 lime

Directions:

Place all of the ingredients into a blender with enough water to cover them and blitz until smooth. Add crushed ice to make your smoothie really refreshing.

Nutrition:

Calories: 180

Fat: 2 g

Carbohydrates: 25 g

Protein: 3 g

Chocolate, Strawberry and Coconut Crush

Preparation time: 5 minutes

Cooking time: 5 minutes

Servings: 1

Ingredients:

100mls (3½fl oz) coconut milk

100g (3½oz) strawberries

1 banana

1 tablespoon 100% cocoa powder or cacao nibs

1 teaspoon matcha powder

Directions:

Toss all of the ingredients into a blender and process them to a creamy consistency.

Add a little extra water if you need to thin it a little. Add crushed ice to make your smoothie really refreshing.

Nutrition:

Calories: 220

Fat: 3 g

Carbohydrates: 30 g

Protein: 5 g

Banana and Kale Smoothie

Preparation time: 5 minutes

Cooking time: 5 minutes

Servings: 1

Ingredients:

50g (2oz) kale

1 banana

200mls (7fl oz) unsweetened soya milk

Directions:

Place all of the ingredients into a blender with enough water to cover them and process until smooth. Add ice to make it really refreshing.

Nutrition:

Calories: 189

Fat: 2 g

Carbohydrates: 25 g

Protein: 3 g

Cranberry and Kale Crush

Preparation time: 5 minutes

Cooking time: 5 minutes

Servings: 1

Ingredients:

75g (3oz) strawberries

50g (2oz) kale

120mls (4fl oz) unsweetened cranberry juice

1 teaspoon chia seeds

½ teaspoon matcha powder

Directions:

Place all of the ingredients into a blender and process until smooth. Add some crushed ice and a mint leaf or two for a really refreshing drink.

Nutrition:

Calories: 213

Fat: 1 g

Carbohydrates: 28 g

Protein: 3 g

Grape, Celery and Parsley Reviver

Preparation time: 5 minutes

Cooking time: 5 minutes

Servings: 1

Ingredients:

75g (3oz) red grapes

3 sticks of celery

1 avocado, de-stoned and peeled

1 tablespoon fresh parsley

½ teaspoon matcha powder

Directions:

Place all of the ingredients into a blender with enough water to cover them and blitz until smooth and creamy. Add crushed ice to make it even more refreshing.

Nutrition:

Calories: 253

Fat: 2 g

Carbohydrates: 35 g

Protein: 3 g

Grapefruit and Celery Blast

Preparation time: 5 minutes

Cooking time: 5 minutes

Servings: 1

Ingredients:

1 grapefruit, peeled

2 stalks of celery

50g (2oz) kale

½ teaspoon matcha powder

Directions:

Place all the ingredients into a blender with enough water to cover them and blitz until smooth.

Add crushed ice to make it even more refreshing.

Nutrition:

Calories: 220

Fat: 1 g

Carbohydrates: 31 g

Protein: 2 g

Tropical Chocolate Delight

Preparation time: 5 minutes

Cooking time: 5 minutes

Servings: 1

Ingredients:

1 mango, peeled & de-stoned

75g (3oz) fresh pineapple, chopped

50g (2oz) kale

25g (1oz) rocket

1 tablespoon 100% cocoa powder or cacao nibs

150mls (5fl oz) coconut milk

Directions:

Place all of the ingredients into a blender and blitz until smooth. You can add a little water if it seems too thick.

Add crushed ice to make it even more refreshing.

Nutrition:

Calories: 289

Fat: 4 g

Carbohydrates: 37 g

Protein: 3 g

Lightning Source UK Ltd.
Milton Keynes UK
UKHW020753030621
384857UK00005B/213